ALCHEMY

The Art of Knowing

Medieval Wisdom

CHRONICLE BOOKS
SAN FRANCISCO

A Labyrinth Book

First published in the United States in 1994 by Chronicle Books.

Design by Meringue Management

The Little Wisdom Library–Medieval Wisdom was produced by Labyrinth Publishing (UK) Ltd. Printed and bound in Italy.

Library of Congress Cataloging-in-Publication Data: Alchemy, Medieval Wisdom.

p. cm. (Medieval Wisdom) Includes bibliographical references.

ISBN 0–8118–0473–9

1. Alchemy —History. I. Chronicle Books (Firm) II. Series.

QD13. A38   1994

540'. 1' 1209 — dc20   93–27406

CIP

Distributed in Canada by Raincoast Books,

112 East Third Avenue, Vancouver, B.C. V5T 1C8

10 9 8 7 6 5 4 3 2 1

Chronicle Books

275 Fifth Street, San Francisco, CA 94103

Introduction

Alchemy and alchemists have always interested the curious, though not always for the same reasons. The prospect of acquiring wealth through the power of transmuting base metals like lead or copper into silver and gold has had an obvious and enduring appeal – few of those who came into contact with the esoteric science were able to resist the riches it claimed to be able to confer. For a more select company, however, the fascination of secret knowledge and the idea of grasping the hidden key to understanding the universe held an even greater appeal, and from the beginning, the practitioners of alchemy claimed that it taught the secret of a spiritual transformation.

Through the alchemical arts, sinful humanity could be transmuted like lead into the pure gold of perfected, transcendent being.

As an art, alchemy is undoubtedly very ancient; its starting point is likely to have been the primitive process by which craftsmen learned, in the second millennium before Christ, to smelt iron and other metals, and hoped to find a way of producing rarer substances like silver and gold. Its basis as a subject for reasoned study was the classification of the elements, or fundamental constituents of matter, by Aristotle and other Greek philosophers under the four headings of fire, air, earth, and water. If all substances were combinations of these four elements, then it must be possible to make any substance out of them by combining them in the right proportions, if only the correct formula could be discovered. It was, therefore, perfectly reasonable, and indeed, given the profit to be made from it, prudent to invest time and resources into the search.

In the closing centuries of the ancient world and in the civilization of Islam, alchemy came to be seen as a body of secret knowledge only to be approached by adepts, of which the mythical Hermes Trismegistus was the first. Most medieval alchemists accepted this, though many scholars with a genuine and rational interest in natural phenomena, like Albertus Magnus and Roger Bacon, conducted experiments and applied analytical methods to a search they regarded as perfectly reasonable. The scientists of the Renaissance and the seventeenth century agreed. It was only when the Greek classification of elements was discredited, in the eighteenth century, that the basis of alchemy crumbled. Paradoxically, modern nuclear physics has once again made the transmutation of metals theoretically possible – by methods not conceivable to the practitioners of the Sacred Art of Alchemy.

In the meanwhile, the quest for the secrets of the transmutation of metals and the Philosopher's Stone stimulated all kinds of scientific progress. Roger Bacon, who devoted ten years to alchemical studies, came to understand the importance of experimental science, neglected by most contemporaries, and, in the course of integrating its results with the doctrines of his predecessors, developed the study of mathematics

Page 4: "The Birth of Mercury" in an alchemist's laboratory. *Page 7:* Wheel of Fortune; 13th C. illumination. *Page 8–9:* The union of opposites that is the goal of esoteric alchemy. *Previous pages:* Dragon feeding on its own tail, from a 15th C. Greek manuscript. *This page:* An alchemist of Persia. *Opposite:* Roger Bacon devoted ten years to the study of alchemy.

as the key to understanding natural phenomena. As a result of Bacon's interest in alchemy, the study of mathematical physics flourished in turn at Oxford, Paris, Padua, and Pisa, laying the basis for the work of Galileo and Newton.

Alchemy, then, was by no means a fruitless quest. On the contrary, in common with other theories about the physical world which were later shown to be unsound – like the "ether" which was believed before 1900 to fill all space – it

was an anvil for numerous fertile lines of study and discovery. The great alchemist Arnald de Villanova learned, as a result of alchemical experiment, methods of counteracting poisons. The first truly experimental science, to which the others owe the first principles of scientific method, was the Sacred Art of Alchemy as it was practiced in the Middle Ages.

Jeremy Catto
Fellow, Oriel College, Oxford

The Sacred Art

*There were the bodies seven and the
spirits four
Which my instructor frequently
rehearsed;
Among the spirits quicksilver came first
And orpiment came second, then he
passed
To sal ammoniac and brimstone last.
As for the seven bodies I should mention,
Here they all are, if they are worth
attention:
Gold for the sun and silver for the moon,
Iron for Mars and quicksilver in tune*

*With Mercury, lead which prefigures
Saturn
And tin for Jupiter. Copper takes the
pattern
Of Venus if you please! This cursed trade
Robs one of all the money one has made
And all one spends on it or round
about it
Will certainly be lost, I cannot doubt it.*

"The Yeoman's Tale"
Geoffrey Chaucer

hen Geoffrey Chaucer
was writing his *Canterbury
Tales* in the late fourteenth
century, alchemy was known by
most people primarily in its guise
of the transmutation of base metals
into gold. The other forms of
alchemy – as medical science and as
a means of spiritual transformation

– were obviously less appealing to
the popular imagination. They
also held less fascination for kings,
who were often more interested in
enriching their coffers than in
healing the sick or in reuniting
the human and the divine. Thus
the Sacred Art of the ancients
became, in medieval Europe,

largely a playground for charlatans and counterfeiters, while a relatively small number of scientists and mystics continued to work in their laboratories, hidden behind veils of secrecy and arcane symbolism.

No one really knows where alchemy began. The most common view is that it originated in Egypt, and certainly some of the earliest recorded history of the Divine Art, as it was also known, comes from that

Previous pages, 14–15: Pedanius Dioscorides, the father of medical pharmacology and science. *Above:* Alchemy is thought by many to have originated in Egypt.

country. According to ancient tradition, the originator of alchemy was Hermes Trismegistus, who is said to have lived some 2500 years before Christ, and who takes the role of teacher in a series of written dialogues of uncertain and mysterious origin. Egypt was called "Khem" at this time, because of the blackness of its soils (*khem* means black); hence the word "alchemy" is derived from this ancient name, and is often known as "the Hermetic art."

Another legend connects alchemy with Adam and Eve at the time

Right: Adam and Eve expelled from the garden, from a 13th C. English manuscript.

A soul that has gained no knowledge of the things that are, and has not come to know their nature, nor to know the Good, but is blind, such a soul is tossed about among the passions which the body breeds; it carries the body as a burden, and is ruled by it instead of ruling it. That is the vice of the soul. On the other hand, the virtue of the soul is knowledge. He who has got knowledge is good and pious; he is already divine....

Hermes Trismegistus, *Libellus X, Corpus Hermeticum*

they were expelled from the Garden of Eden. According to the legend, an angel at the gate took pity on the two as they were leaving, and instructed them in the secrets of alchemy and astrology. As they descended from the spiritual realm to the material world, the secrets Adam and Eve had been given would also change, eventually becoming astronomy and chemistry. But they would be able to remember the spiritual source of these material sciences in the sciences of astrology and alchemy. And by virtue of this remembering, and diligent practice, they would eventually

Alchemies are here prohibited, and those who practice them or procure them being done are punished. They must forfeit to the public treasury for the benefit of the poor as much genuine gold and silver as they have manufactured of the false or adulterated metal. If they have not sufficient means for this the penalty may be changed to another at the discretion of the judge, and they shall be considered criminals.

Pope John XXII, 1317

be able to return to the Garden.

One esoteric tradition holds that the science of alchemy was brought to Egypt by refugees from the sinking continent of Atlantis; still others connect the origin of the word alchemy with the Hebrew word *chamaman,* or *hamaman,* meaning a sacred mystery not to be revealed to the general populace, but to be treasured by the priesthood as a religious secret. Certainly, for many centuries, alchemy (and, in fact, nearly all

Opposite: Persian astrologers like Ibn 'Arabi, developer of this system of correspondences, had a profound influence on medieval alchemists.

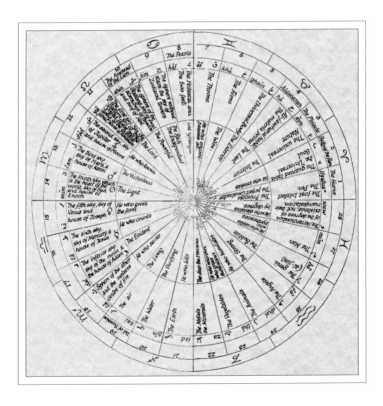

science and learning) was the exclusive province of the priesthood, and its secrets were transmitted only to initiates.

Whatever its origins, most scholars of the subject agree that alchemy was based on spiritual and philosophical concepts. Those concepts certainly predated Christianity, and were, therefore, "pagan" in the eyes of the medieval church – a good reason for the alchemists of the Middle Ages to wrap their work in the costume of metallurgy, and thereby hope to avoid being persecuted as heretics.

The fundamental premise of alchemy is that there are precise correspondences between the visible and invisible worlds, the worlds of matter and spirit, inner and outer, heaven and earth. According to the alchemical view, everything – plant, animal, mineral – contains a "seed" of divinity, and this seed can be developed through application of certain principles of learning and culture. In philosophical terms, then, alchemy is the art of transforming the base metal of ignorance into the gold of wisdom, or divinity. Furthermore, according to alchemy, the material world is a reflection of the spiritual world,

Left: Mandrake from an illustration in an Arab manuscript. One branch of medieval alchemy concerned itself primarily with healing.

and should work according to the same principles. It should be possible, therefore, to transform the grosser physical substances into more refined ones, or literally to transform base metals into gold.

ingredient in the science of alchemy is the alchemist himself. He or she must have the power to attract and make use of the invisible spiritual ingredient, the "divine spark," that brings about

The secret of success in this latter process, however, is the secret that has eluded so many practitioners of the art through the ages. The most important secret the desired transformation. In other words, the alchemist must be, as Hermes Trismegistus was reported to be, able to "imitate the work of the gods."

Above: Hermes Trismegistus, master alchemist. *Right:* The background in the box is an Italian painting symbolizing the beginning of the alchemical work.

*S*hall all men teach? What manner
of people may this science reach,
And which is the true science of alchemy
of old fathers called blessed and holy?

It must need be taught from mouth to mouth
And also he shall (be he ever so loath)
Regard it with sacred and most dreadful oath.
So blood and blood may have no part
But only virtue winneth this Holy Art.

Thomas Norton, *15th Century English Alchemist*

The Alchemists
and
Their Search

To penetrate the many veils of secrecy and symbolism surrounding the practice of alchemy in medieval times would take a lifetime of study – and even then, the investigator would probably be not much nearer to the truth of what was really happening in alchemical laboratories than when the investigation began. Much of the written literature of alchemy is so convoluted and full of riddles that it is nearly impossible to make sense of it. In fact, the word 'gibberish' is derived from the name of one Arab alchemist, Jabir (or Geber), because of the apparently nonsensical nature of

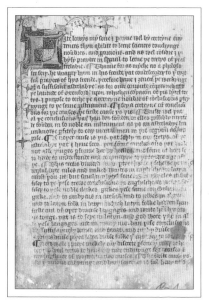

Previous pages: An illustration of the second stage of the Great Work, according to George Ripley. *Above:* A page from Chaucer's treatise on the Astrolabe.

his writings. Furthermore, some alchemical manuscripts are attributed to authors who either did not exist, or who had died long before the manuscripts were supposedly authored by them!

The practice of authoring alchemical treatises using pseudonyms most likely arose out of the fact that a number of important public and religious figures were engaged in alchemical studies, and did not wish to be ridiculed or persecuted. In addition, it was a common practice among alchemists to weave together legend, factual history, and alchemical secrets, and to publish these allegorical tales as a way of passing on their knowledge to other adepts and initiates with whom they might not have been personally acquainted. With this caution in mind, then, we can sample the works of a few of the more famous medieval alchemists, in search of the common threads of Sacred Art underlying their mysterious writings. Along with these writings, we can examine some of the fantastical tales that so often surround the lives of the alchemists, and gain a glimpse into their contribution to medieval wisdom.

Albertus Magnus

Born in 1193, Albertus Magnus (Albertus Groot) became a Dominican in 1222, and later taught philosophy and theology in Hildesheim and Paris. In Paris, Thomas Aquinas was one of his students, and, according to legend, was the one to whom Albertus passed on his alchemical formulae before he died. According to the same story, Thomas Aquinas destroyed an "android" who was the product of his teacher's life work. This creature had been created from certain combinations of metals and secret ingredients, and was vested with the power of thought and speech. Thomas, being a pious sort of fellow, destroyed the android because he considered it to be the work of the devil.

Towards the end of his life, Albertus Magnus left his teaching duties and again took up monastic life, this time in Cologne, where he remained until his death in 1280.

One fascinating legend surrounds this particular part of the alchemist's life. It is said that he invited a number of nobles, including William II, Count of Holland, to attend a garden party at the Cologne monastery – in the middle of the German winter! The invited guests were aghast at the idea, but accepted his invitation anyway. As they sat down to eat, Albertus uttered a few words, the snow disappeared, and the garden was filled with flowers, singing birds, and the warm breezes of summer. As soon as the feast was over, the wintry landscape returned.

Opposite background: An Arab alchemist consults the tables of Hermes; late 14th C. illustration.

RULES FOR THE PRACTICING ALCHEMIST

First. He should be discreet and silent, revealing to no one the result of his operations.

Second. He should reside in a private house in an isolated situation.

Third. He should choose his days and hours for labor with discretion.

Fourth. He should have patience, diligence, and perseverance.

Fifth. He should perform according to fixed rules.

Sixth. He should use only vessels of glass or glazed earthenware.

Seventh. He should be sufficiently rich to bear the expenses of his art.

Eighth. He should avoid having anything to do with princes and noblemen.

Albertus Magnus

Roger Bacon

An Englishman, and a contemporary of Albertus Magnus, Roger Bacon taught philosophy in Paris at the same time as Albertus. He developed a process for refining saltpeter, is credited with inventing gunpowder in Europe, and published extensive works on metallurgy and other natural sciences. Today, Bacon is known as the greatest experimental scientist of the Middle Ages. But in his own lifetime, he was convicted of heresy and imprisoned, where he spent the last fifteen years of his life before his death in 1292.

George Ripley

George Ripley is said to have been another disciple of Albertus Magnus, but since he lived almost 200 years later, it seems unlikely. In any case, he spent the early part of his life in a monastery, and then travelled for some time throughout Europe, visiting the Isle of Rhodes during his journeys.

Above: The knight symbolizes the unifying principle, and the colors in his armor represent all the stages of the alchemical process. *Opposite:* The alchemical Wheel of Fortune makes its way into a 14th C. illumination of the Bible.

There, he lived for some months with the warrior-monks of the Order of St. John of Jerusalem, whose job was to look after pilgrims to the Holy Land while it was occupied by the Saracens. Ripley was apparently quite taken with these knights and their mission, and reportedly gave vast sums of money to help them in their wars against the Turks.

On his return to his native England, Ripley became a member of the Carmelite order where he resumed the alchemical studies that had occupied him in his youth. There, he completed his most famous work, *The Compound of Alchymie Conteining Twelve Gates*. This treatise was published in 1475, and was dedicated to King Edward IV. Written in verse, it outlines the twelve processes needed to develop the magnum opus, or Philosopher's Stone, which might be said to be the physical counterpart to the mysterious spiritual ingredient needed for the process of transmutation. Ripley's work, which he described as akin to "the gates of a castle which a philosopher must enter," led later scholars to associate alchemy with

King Solomon of the Bible, and to argue that these same twelve steps can be found encoded in the verses of *the Song of Solomon*.

Arnald de Villanova

Arnald de Villanova began his studies with the Dominicans, where his primary interest was in the area of medicine. He apparently also studied philosophy with Albertus Magnus in Paris, and thereafter became famous as a great physician. For a time, he studied in Montpellier, which was a center for the teaching of Arabian medical sciences, and afterwards became the chief physician at the

> Although we write primarily for the edification of the disciples of the art, we also write for the mystification of those owls and bats which can neither bear the splendor of the sun nor the light of the moon.
>
> George Ripley

Court of Aragon in Spain. Throughout his life, it seemed that the authorities were torn between respect for Arnald's considerable intelligence and healing abilities, and suspicion of his association with the heresies of the infidels and alchemists. There are repeated stories of "religious troubles," and in Paris he was once thrown into prison, and all his books were burned. But the Bishop of Paris helped to secure his release, and Arnald went to Italy where, over a period of time, he served as physician to two different popes and the King of Sicily.

He is credited with introducing the idea of the "vital principle," or "quintessence" to define the mysterious spiritual force required for the successful practice of alchemy. His application of alchemical principles to medicine led him to be one of the first to use alcohol for making preparations of drugs, and his efforts undoubtedly laid the groundwork for later alchemists of medicine like Cornelius Agrippa and Paracelsus in the sixteenth century.

Bernard of Treves

The story of Bernard is the story of one who devoted his entire life to seeking the Philosopher's Stone and the secret of transmuting base metals into gold. He was born into wealth so had no problem in setting up a laboratory and attracting many helpers of lesser means. A tireless and single-pointed seeker, Bernard also travelled throughout Europe, the Mediterranean and the Middle East in his search for those who knew the Sacred Art. Each time he heard tales that some experimenter had discovered the secret, he would set out for the city where the alchemist lived, usually to find out that there was no real substance to the story.

Finally, at the age of eighty, Bernard had squandered almost his entire fortune in his fruitless search, and retired to the island of Rhodes. There, he found a merchant who was willing to loan him money against the last of his estates, and Bernard constructed a new laboratory where he ate, slept, and worked his way through the last of his money, after which he was literally facing starvation. Here, the legend says, was where he discovered the secret of transmutation at last. He spent the final three years of his life enjoying the wealth it brought him. Bernard himself, however, says in his memoirs that he never did manage to find the Philosopher's Stone, but he found something much more important–the secret of contentment.

Nicholas Flamel

One of the most romantic stories in the history of alchemy is that of Nicholas Flamel. According to legend, he lived in Paris during the fourteenth century, where he worked as a scrivener. During the performance of these duties, he came across a very large and very ancient book, bound in brass and written on papyrus leaves gilded with gold.

The writing on the cover was in a strange and unknown language, and the book was organized into three sections of seven leaves each. Strange images and figures were painted on the seventh leaf of each section, including a virgin being swallowed by serpents, a serpent being crucified on a cross, and a beautiful landscape watered by fountains from which many writhing serpents emerged.

Nicholas spent many years in deciphering the writings and the symbols of the book which, of course, included instruction in the process of transmuting metals. His difficulty was that the secret ingredient, the Philosopher's Stone, was encoded within the paintings, and these he could not figure out. Finally he found a doctor, a Christianized Jew, who was able to help him decode the secret of the magical stone. Nicholas returned to his laboratories in Paris in the company of the doctor, who conveniently fell sick and died on the way. But after three years of experimentation, Nicholas Flamel finally succeeded in producing the "prime agent" of transmutation, and he and his wife became quite wealthy as a result. By the beginning of

Previous pages, 35: An alchemist from a miniature by Lucas van Leiden. *Page 37:* The "generation" stage of the alchemical process; 15th C. illustration of George Ripley's work. *Opposite:* The Wheel of Fortune in an illustration for a 14th C. French version of the *Romance of the Rose.*

the fifteenth century, they had founded fourteen hospitals, built three chapels, endowed seven churches, and restored cemeteries in Paris and Boulogne. Thus, they proved themselves truly worthy of the secret ingredient of alchemy, by using the proceeds from its discovery to help humanity rather than solely to enrich themselves.

Alchemical
Symbolism

Obscure and contradictory as it often is, the alchemical literature does contain certain common symbols that can be identified, and they are presented here as an indication of the basic principles that have guided alchemists in their search for spiritual and scientific wisdom.

Within the processes of alchemy, there are three primary chemical substances: mercury, sulphur, and salt. In addition, there is a fourth substance, which is always portrayed as a mysterious "life

Previous pages: Persian illustration showing the phases of the moon. *Right:* Alchemical symbols in this 16th C. illustration of Virgil's *Aeneid* include the Tree of Life and the Birds of Sublimation. *Opposite:* The beginning of the Great Work; 17th C. illustration for George Ripley's text.

principle." In early Egyptian writings, this principle was called "Azoth." Azoth was the measureless spirit of life and came from the outer regions of the universe to be poured into the four elements of earth, air, fire and water. According to the Egyptians, these four elements flowed from the throne of God, passing on their way through the Garden of Eden, where they accumulated the spiritual earth, or the "Dust of Aphar," out of which God originally made the body of man.

Aristotle agreed with this ancient Egyptian classification of four basic elements, if not the fables surrounding their origins, and further defined the assumptions of scientific inquiry for many centuries to follow. Essentially, it was believed that these four elements reacted with one another to produce metals, for example, and all forms of life on Earth. If man could replicate these interactions in a controlled fashion, then he would be able not only to create gemstones and precious metals, but animal and plant life itself.

It must be understood that each of the four elements also had a symbolic value. Many ancient cultures believed that mankind's first instruction in the sciences had come from creatures who emerged from the sea (water).

Air represented the spirit, and was the medium that united all living beings. Fire caused all motion (heat) and, therefore, was at the root of all change. And

TABLES OF ALCHEMICAL CORRESPONDENCES

The Four Corners of Creation:	East	South	West	North
The Parts of the Cherubim:	Man	Lion	Eagle	Bull
The Four Seasons:	Spring	Summer	Autumn	Winter
The Stages of Existence:	Birth	Growth	Maturity	Decay
Man's Constitution:	Spirit	Soul	Mind	Body

earth, though it was not an active principle, was the receptive vehicle required for all these other things to take place.

The first alchemists shared, in common with the scientists who followed them, a quest for an orderly and coherent way of relating all the diverse elements of their universe. Once the elements had been clearly

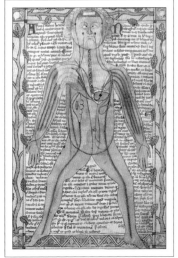

defined, then presumably one could experiment with their proportions and interactions, and discover the underlying principles of creation, evolution and transmutation.

Within the practice of alchemy, furthermore, there was always a kind of practical expectation which took the form of a chemical substance. This substance

Above: A 13th C. view of the arteries in a man's body.
Opposite: The alchemists were among the first scientists in Europe. Their attempts to understand the order inherent in the universe are reflected in tables like this one, and the one on the following page.

was seen as a mix of mystical understanding and chemical materials, and the hoped-for result was a "universal medicine," an elixir of life that would ultimately not only cure all physical ills but resolve man's connection with God and the universe. All religious, medical, chemical, and astrological knowledge was enlisted by the alchemist in the service of making this ultimate discovery.

Alchemical formulae were also closely associated with astrology, and each stage of the alchemical work was believed to be influenced by the movements of the heavens. During most of the Middle Ages, astrology and astronomy were not separate studies but one and the same, so that the position of

ASTROLOGICAL CORRESPONDENCES TO ALCHEMICAL PROCESSES

Aries - Calcination	**Leo** - Digestion	**Sagittarius** - Incineration
Taurus - Congelation	**Virgo** - Distillation	**Capricorn** - Fermentation
Gemini - Fixation	**Libra** - Sublimation	**Aquarius** - Multiplication
Cancer - Dissolution	**Scorpio** - Separation	**Pisces** - Projection

the planets in the solar system was studied both in relation to science and humanity.

Each time an alchemical process was undertaken, the various positions of the planets had to be determined so that each step of the work could be completed with the help of the most favorable astrological influences. This undoubtedly added to the complexity of alchemy and confounded many of the experiments, because the science of astronomy and astrology in Europe at the time was as primitive and inaccurate as that of chemistry itself.

Right: Medieval Persian illustration symbolizing Saturn.

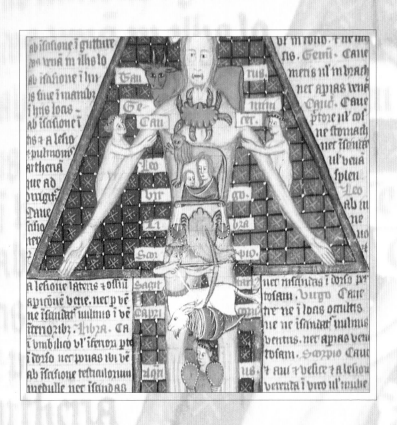

In the Holy Fire

Ultimately, the real object of alchemical experimentation was that of creating the Philosopher's Stone, the physical vehicle for the "divine spark" necessary to the process of transmutation. One of the most potent and romantic of alchemical symbols was the belief that if a tiny piece of the Philosopher's Stone were placed on the surface of water, the complete process of creation would take place in miniature, so that the entire story of the unfolding of the universe could be perceived by the experimenter. This extraordinary idea was echoed in the concept of reading the future through water-gazing. For example, the sixteenth century prophet Nostradamus was said to have used such alchemical devices in making his prophecies. Sitting at night in a candle-lit loft, using various herbal mixtures and alchemical processes, he would gaze into water in a brass bowl, uttering ancient occult words and passing into deep trances. The result was *The Centuries,* a ten-volume group of almost a thousand predictions which are still believed by some to foretell accurately the future of mankind right through to the thirty-eighth century.

Previous page: Zodiacal man, a painting found in late 14th C. English astrological works.
Opposite: A symbolic representation of the birth of the Philosopher's Stone.

In all this magical construction, the alchemist would have had many excuses for failure. One of the most stringent requirements was that the process must operate simultaneously in all the "four worlds" of God, man, the elements and the chemicals. Any one experiment, undertaken in any case according to the most complex set of procedures, had to be successful in all four worlds, or the alchemist could work all his life without success.

One of the legendary requirements of the alchemical process was, according to some practitioners of the art, to say a prayer to the "ultimate" alchemist – God – before starting the experiments. One such prayer, translated here from Old German, went as follows:

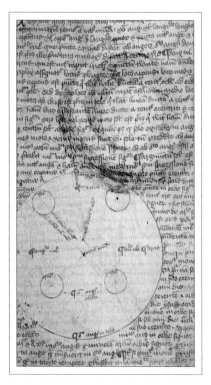

"O holy and hallowed Trinity. Cause me to sink into the abyss of Thy limitless eternal Fire, for only in that Fire can the mortal nature of man be changed into humble dust, while the new body of the salt union lies in the light. Oh, melt me and transmute me in this Thy holy Fire, so that on the day at Thy command the fiery waters of the Holy Spirit draw me out from the dark dust, giving me new birth and making me alive with his breath. May I also be exalted through the humble humility of Thy Son, rising through His assistance out of the dust and ashes and changing into a pure spiritual body of rainbow colors and ashes and changing into a

Left: Medieval treatise on the planets of the solar system. *Above:* "Magician at Work," from a 14th C. Persian manuscript.

pure spiritual body of rainbow colors like unto the transparent, crystal-like, paradisiacal gold, that my own nature may be redeemed and purified like the elements before me in these glasses and bottles. Diffuse me in the waters of life as though I were in the wine cellar of the eternal Solomon. Here the fire of Thy love will receive new fuel and will blaze forth so that no streams can extinguish it. Through the aid of this divine fire, may I in the end be found worthy to be called into the illumination of the righteous. May I then be sealed up with the light of the new world that I may also attain

unto the immortality and glory where there shall be no more alternation of light and darkness. Amen."

Those who actually succeeded in their efforts to achieve the creation of the Philosopher's Stone were thought always to remain hidden from the rest of the world, for as they became enlightened by their efforts so they effectively disappeared from normal human sight. They were also said to be members of a kind of holy group which remained in touch with one another but not with anyone else in the world. None of

Left: The "maturation" phase of the alchemical process; 15th C. illustration of George Ripley's work.

them were permitted to reveal the secret of their success, or to put the true secrets in writing.

The successful alchemist was permitted to appoint one assistant, who became a kind of sorcerer's apprentice and was

the only one to whom the alchemist might teach his art. It is said that during the sixteenth to eighteenth centuries there were a large number of al-chemists who app-eared here and there (perhaps seeking apprentices) and mysteriously disap-peared again, often without warning. These alchemists were said also to possess the secret of immortality, which they had gained from the use of the elixirs they had discovered in their work. Presumably they still live, hidden behind the veil of their magical abilities.

Above: The "purging of the earth" phase of the alchemical process. *Opposite:* The background in the box is a 14th C. prognosticatory calendar. *Following page:* The "resurrection" phase of the alchemical process.

The path to immortality is hard, and only a few find it. The rest await the Great Day when the wheels of the universe shall be stopped and the immortal sparks shall escape from the sheaths of substance. Woe unto those who wait, for they must return again, unconscious and unknowing, to the seed-ground of the stars, and await a new beginning.

The Divine Pymander of Hermes Trismegistus

Burkhardt, Titus. *Alchemy: Science of the Cosmos, Science of the Soul.* William Stoddart, trans. Stuart & Watkins, London, 1967.

Caron, Marcel, and Serge Hutin. *The Alchemists.* Helen R. Lane, trans. Evergreen Books, San Francisco, 1971.

Clymer, Reuben Swinbirne. *Alchemy and the Alchemists.* Philosophical Publishing Co., London, 1907.

Hall, Manly P. *The Secret Teachings of All Ages: An Encyclopedic Outline of Masonic, Hermetic, Cabbalistic, and Rosicrucian Philosophy.* Philosophical Research Society, Los Angeles, 1975.

Hermetica: the Writings attributed to Hermes Trismegistus, Walter Scott, ed. and trans. Solos Press, U.K., 1992.

Barrett, T. *The Lives of the Alchemystical Philosophers.* Lackington, Allen & Co., U.K., 1814.

Fabricus, J. *The Medieval Alchemist and their Royal Art.* 2nd ed., Aquarian (Harper Collins), Wellingborough, 1989.

Hall, A. R. *The Revolution in Science, 1500-1750.* London: Longmans, 1983.

Hudson, John. *The History of Chemistry.* London: MacMillan, 1992.

Holmyard, E. J. *Alchemy.* New York: Penguin/Dover, 1990.

Taylor, F. S. *The Alchemists.* London: Heinemann, 1951.

Salzberg, H. W. *From Caveman to Chemist.* Washington D.C.: American Chemical Society, 1990.

ACKNOWLEDGMENTS

Every effort has been made to trace all present copyright holders of the material used in this book, whether companies or individuals. Any omission is unintentional, and we will be pleased to correct errors in future editions of this book.

Text acknowledgments:

p. 16: Chaucer, Geoffrey. *The Canterbury Tales.* Nevill Coghill, trans. Penguin, U.K., 1977.

pp. 19, 34, 44, 46: Hall, Manly P. *The Secret Teachings of all Ages: An Encyclopedic Outline of Masonic, Hermetic, Cabbalistic and Rosicrucian Philosophy.* Philosophical Research Society, Los Angeles, 1975.

p. 25: Clymer, Reuben Swinbirne. *Alchemy and the Alchemists.* Philosophical Publishing Co., London, 1907.

pp. 31, 53: Barrett, T. *The Lives of the Alchemystical Philosophers.* Lackington, Allen & Co., U.K., 1814.

p. 57: *Hermetica: the Writings attributed to Hermes Trismegistus.* Walter Scott, ed. and trans. Solos Press, U.K., 1992.

Picture acknowledgments:
Zentralbibliothek, Zurich; Page: 4.
Stadtbibliothek, Vadiana; Page: 8.
Bodleian Library; Pages: 7, 12, 13 14, 18, 22, 26, 28, 33, 37, 39, 40, 43, 45, 47, 48, 52, 53, 54, 56, 57, 58.
Biblioteca Apostolica Vaticano; Pages: 25, 31.
British Library; Pages: 35, 42, 51.